CHIRP

HYSTERICAL BOOKS

CHIRP

HYSTERICAL BOOKS
TALLAHASSEE, FL 2019

Copyright © Su Zi 2019
All rights reserved under
International and Pan-American Copyright Conventions.

No portion of this book may be reproduced in any form without the written permission of the publisher, except by a reviewer, who may quote brief passages in connection with a review for a magazine or newspaper.

Chirp by Su Zi — First Edition

ISBN — 978-0-940821-13-2
Library of Congress Cataloging Card Number — 2019948606

Hysterical Books is dedicated wholly to the
publication and appreciation of fine poetry and other literary genres.

HYSTERICAL BOOKS
1506 Wekewa Nene
Tallahassee Florida

Published in the United States by Hysterical Books
Tallahassee, Florida • First Edition, 2019
hystericalbooks.com
hystericalbooks@gmail.com

Dedication:

You Know Who You Are

Every day, observations were made about local bird activity—in a sort of 19thC field note fashion—and translated into these formed stanzas. Effort was made for correct species identification, and grateful thanks are made to the Cornell website for confirmation of auditory evidence.

CHIRP

this mid-winter warmth
so spring, ought to bring rain
but no, just the wind

cold came with little
rain, just pockmarks in sand and
 spikes in horses' fur

ice when the moon wanes:
Cranes curtsey, their exact walk
paired, to this year's nest

frost insults the dawn
making vapors from water
rising, as Bluebirds flirt.

sun crests the treeline
Cranes, crows call into echo
until Doves are heard

solar azimuth still
too south, yet soundscape is rich
with Scrubjays and Wrens

lemons that flutter
flitting: Warblers : ocher grass
of winter pastures

she is weaving a
cradle, choosing found fur, dried
flowers: expectant.

we smelled rain at dark
dawn brought darkening of sand
slow burn, slow screaming

these hands are small, square
not restless but too busy
to be manicured

morning glistens from
the midnight rain. even blue Scrub
Jays hark hope of spring

love lorn Dove : sad flute
 yet delight: Yellow Chested Chat
 rare. my mute reward

what is memory
pencils of light through blinds
a word that lingers

triangle of Ducks
the fur of horses drifts to earth
cities are not all

local dialect
can be heard in birds, until
road noise gets louder.

the lust of the birds
a symphony. in stillness
trees sleep in pink dusk

Woodpecker agrees
 yup-yup: a due south wind brings
silver-clouded storm.

at noon, the chill creeps,
touching, as if it loves us.
making Crows timid.

contrails are revealed
as hash against perfection.
Wrens seem more busy

dark to dark we are
in the arctic wind. years now
touch and a calm eye

sharp light, sharp cold, wind
lone Robin falls silent when
Hawk she cries looking.

mamma Crane , a gray
oval, demure on her nest
she thus honors me

white head, white tail glint.
brown wings a meter of grace
in elegant sky.

raccoon argument
makes worry about Crane nest.
fragile survival

Mocking bird returns
his extensive repertoire
is full, round and rich.

intricate soundscape
even Robins visit now
this morning so sweet.

mama Hawk argues
with Crow. high surf of clouds brings
wind of distant blooms

gray is the mist now
falling. A lone Woodpecker
trills without response.

midnight rain, full moon:
bright wings wake hues, oldest oaks
dress first in flowers.

Cardinal is first
in gray before dawn; with light
finally comes rain

power lines, county road:
Bald eagles perch in their aerie
witnessing our rush.

Bright Prairie Warblers,
Bluebirds vivid when sun crests
slowly greening trees

gregarious now
Crows crowd and glutton all seeds
leaving Wrens forlorn.

the ocean of air
is loud and lusty today
thus brave are Sparrows.

gray, cold and silent,
a morning for hiding; lone
is the Crow, the Dove.

triangles of ice
water trough, yet sun brings song
Cardinal's jazz riff.

mama Crane has left
her nest; an oval absent.
Was the dawn's shriek hers?

three Wood Thrushes perch
bamboo hides Cardinal's nest
mom still hunts later.

oblong, my life's joy
between hand yet mystery
you who were once tree

sun's touch is deeper
in rising azimuth, and
there, suddenly, Swallows.

sun breath while mare eats,
soft shuffle of seeds teasing
the bold, boy Bluebirds.

in saint petersburg
Heron perches hawthorn, bold
grace at rare book fair.

belly white in flight
in the sky at first light over
pasture rare Kite you.

Magnolia Warbler
Least Flycatcher busy, near
rewarding stillness.

been this long since rain,
morning mist thickening , and
Robin suddenly.

cold returns as if
hungry, despite more greening
and Ibis nesting.

first light, a lone Duck;
then, as darkness rises pink
west, sliver, comet.

mist rises from ponds
sun's azimuth almost east
red bird, golden light.

Marsh Hawk—Cooper's Hawk—
russet bomb to cattail thatch
Anhinga weeps shock.

fog makes privacy
this silver morning, just
horses, dogs, Scrubjay.

Thrushes, Ground Doves, Cranes
strolling triad, lady bird
silver-gold morning.

equinox soundscape
Scrubjays, Cardinals, and Crows,
shift in air to sweet

silver sky at noon.
Lake Bower toms fan display
to coy, demure hens.

Momma Mockingbird
so pregnant, hops air in arcs
Royal Hawks circle.

Heart Mare leaves behind
palm of grain. Lady and Sir
Redbird's eager gift.

Pileated riffs
beat on old Live Oak that
blooms. all shall now sing.

amaryllis blooms
Equinox full moon. in wind
Horses bend their heads.

median between
midnight and dawn, there's only
Whippoorwill's comfort.

this year, cold too long
fists of wind, joyous surf for
Grasshopper Sparrows.

Heron's silent flight
alone against the pale cold
morning in March, still.

in sudden stillness
Osprey watches from bare branch
Deer appear at fence.

Moon shadowed with wan
west, while in gold fire Bluebird
shows himself and sings.

Ishtar, East Star, arms
of water, absent of birds
except one lone Tern.

Mockingbird, Redbird
 duet all day: call—echo;
April sun blazes.

this weary body
listens to clouds, blue-gray, that
lap, at last, from south.

blue surf from west where
beyond horizon The Gulf
sends storms, hidden songs.

crystalline light, air
whose voice the lone note clear
others orchestrate.

welcome: Woodpecker
speckled tux, round red head;
twilight's Whippoorwill.

roseate sunset
last lone call of Cranes and Crows
ebbing the wind.

curled eternal
no more rattlesnake, Possum;
Vulture stands watch.

late to bloom: Birches
Crepe Myrtles, Swamp Tupelo
branches purple now.

new leaves glow under
ambling clouds gray with promise.
time past, parents wed.

at morning, scrubjays
collective conversation
matches the gray wind.

prodigal, their white
elliptical strut hunts bugs
no regrets, Egrets.

afternoon, Mockingbird
Griot of his odyssey
some lost, ancient songs.

morning glistens from
midnight rain. Thrush , mouth full, stares;
steps into bamboo.

in morning's thick mist,
Peeping Ducks lazy eight and
settle; shrunken pond.

Mamma Kildear flaps
in road dust, chirring, trying
distract Crows from nest.

even Crepe Myrtle
unfurls leaves, Mockingbird
chants mythology.

Ground Dove, Mourning Dove:
sweet alto songs, ovals of
grace, rain jeweled grass.

in rain, Crows greet gray
light; Pony bends his head, hears
Woodpecker laughing.

before the fading
of night to blue-gray first light;
all voices silent.

again, the misty
morning; Peeping Ducks swirl low
counterpoint to Cranes.

his is yellow eye
in befriending Brown Thrasher
stillness is reward.

Hawk weeping for mate
casts circles of shadow; rust
corpse, so light, so soft.

Peeping Ducks surf
first fist of gold over trees,
greeting the Horses.

Mother Ocean, feet
brought to your warm, briny kiss
happy birthday, me.

Anclote: Dolphins curve;
bird key—Puffins, Pipers, Terns,
Pelican triad.

Ocean teaches Sky;
so embrace of ancient Live Oak,
of Red Hawk is home.

thunder to the north,
but smell of rain is distant;
sunset's long shadows.

rising mist from rain
after dark; no Owl at night,
but Crane calls from swamp.

Mockingbird chases
Crow: low flight under low clouds;
as are Peeping Ducks.

Lady Cardinal
fussy in rain that pleases
Great Snowy Egret.

midmorning, Wood Stork
in the swamp across the gate
stands solo and still.

over grasses' glow
gray recedes to silver, trees
reseed; golden day.

Mockingbird and Hawk
patrol and hunt waves of wind
in the bright morning.

Woodpecker's red head
inquires of poplar tree, what
be this sad struggle.

midnight sings of frogs,
beyond pastures, where trees dream
maybe there's an Owl.

Vulture flaunts flight skill
on breezes that curlicue
over new flowers.

throbbing of fever
fear of deafness: to lose Jay's
call, Ground Dove's twitter

in the long shadows
Mourning Dove and Mockingbird
make their last report.

Bluebird sways, singing
uppermost edge of bamboo,
then is a flash gone.

at Moss Bluff, lone Goose :
ebony head, long white throat,
marching with soft bleats.

he dances for her
still, in bayou's long shadows
of morning in May.

sun north of west now:
lovebugs are silent, but the
cicadas not.

always Mockingbird
serious sentry: rasping
at Crows; ornate song.

eyre of Osprey,
Bald Eagle on power poles
peek the fledgling heads.

Indigo Bunting
knotting air over bamboo
heard for mornings later.

lone Duck, where's your flock
your pink breast glows in morning
solo circles now.

river has too few
creatures of air and water
one last Moorhen now.

each song has a time:
bright light, bright flight of hawk call,
or early dew all.

Whippoorwill and Owl
of the night when blue deepens;
gratitude for rain.

moment's steady stare
Thrasher meets gaze,
shares the space, a friendly gift.

woven sun and rain
at noon: sweet notes from Bluebird,
Cardinal, and frog.

one Red-winged Blackbird
appears storm's edge, stays some days
in cattails of pond.

first light fog, and then
in Candler, parent Cranes stroll
beside half-grown twins.

pink full moon fades west;
Thrush, small green frog limp in beak
golden eye and pause.

soldier boy sunday:
last night, neighbors shot their guns;
now, only Doves cry.

gone are the Turtles,
Gators, Fish from Lake Weir, just
six Seagulls swimming.

gladiola blooms
from forgotten bulb; sweet breeze
Woodpecker's soft trill.

Scrubjays call quartet
from Oak tree that had a stroke:
part nest holes, part live.

sun through mist maybe
rain: Lady Cardinal's seeds,
few bites before flight.

if afternoon rains,
Peeping Ducks embroider air
elaborately.

Mockingbird insists
dominion: erudition
of song his power.

after every rain,
when frogs fill light with their chant,
one Wood Stork only.

one Bluebird perches
as Scrub Jays call a morning chant;
clouds flower silent.

sun silver circle;
Hawk wing's tip silver circle;
storm too is silver.

morning; first named storm;
she is tan hesitation
out late in wet green.

Osprey babies learn
flight—parents' voices an arc—
thus many white wings.

long is the light now ,
rain band arrives, drenches, fades so
vivid now green June.

this is the rising,
the apex of gold, the gift;
yes, Cardinal knows.

casting seed circles
afternoon's edge, Cardinal
flutters up nearby.

they offer treaty:
to witness their grace for the
safeguard of their children.

one well-traveled Crow
speaks Seagull, has loud meow;
and his tribal call.

Cranes—slow, regal stride—
together up the hammock
accept offered corn.

they ask now, the Cranes,
with soft chuckles and nearness;
then, grace as they eat.

when silver skies send
golden oval to rich grass,
Ground Doves swirl churring.

the long evening
Cardinals' call and response
under rumbling clouds.

unseen Woodpecker
chuckles from the cool shadows
of a damp morning.

pink east, light retreats
this sapphire hour past green flash
Whippoorwill's question.

softest of shadows
cicadas pulse steel chants;
Cranes call long twilight

Blue jay calls solo
against deep, rolling voices
clouds hue of his wings.

silver mist morning;
then, tender gift rain this
the sacred solstice.

their bodies stillness,
yet not, ever unfurling
longest light, large moon.

respectful distance
their orange eyes unfaltering
Cranes, two, in request.

alone against sky,
Snowy Egret drifts downward;
forlorn cry from reeds

edges of the light,
wax and wan, rise and set; edge
trees to sky is gray.

noon: curve and vector
Snowy Egret returns from west,
bringing another.

Pine Island: Blackbirds
in oleanders, but one
Gull, one black Swallow.

two Cranes: he stands guard;
she, with dainty sewing, eats;
he escorts away.

June ends, yet they dance;
great, gray wings enough open
to float, to hover.

too few against sky
their gentle pinks and peeping,
alas, Whistling Ducks

quiet under clouds
only trees breathing in wind;
bird absence echoes.

no flight feathers yet;
unbalanced stump tail, stubby wings,
Mockingbird in grass.

this year's children learn
the song of their tribe, the song
of air after rain.

this moist midnight when
old scars ache, comfort is from
Cranes who trill softly.

parking lot Raven
pokes greasy paper, then limps,
then not: threat is gone

Cattle Egrets learn
tractors spook meaty treats;
amber crowns, their eyes.

Cardinal insists
his song, tireless ; shadows
shorten, heat rises.

Cranes come for breakfast:
unusual; also, two
Mockingbirds' song duel.

his unceasing song,
met gaze, wide repertoire, rage;
mate's feathers in grass.

rain at four o clock,
as old; then, soprano songs,
Morning Dove's alto.

winged red men: friends,
flying synchronized arcs,
playful, Cardinals.

no Owl calls midnight,
no Whippoorwill sweetens dark;
birds are gone from night.

minute by minute,
life by life, one where many
a lone Crow on pole.

clouds return pre-noon,
locusts' choral rattle
one Woodpecker's song.

after rain: one, one,
Great Egret, Wood Stork hunt frogs;
gray sky, V-tail—Kite.

river's headwaters,
one Osprey clutching a perch;
later another.

six Crows come to feast
on hoof dust, leave corn untouched;
pyramids offered.

Ibis stroll damp grass
one mud-hued baby follows
mirroring momma.

after rain, soft glow,
luminosity of plants;
first voice, Mourning Dove.

day of thick, gray rain;
at evening, the two Cranes
calling and strolling.

overcast, tall grass
Woodpecker's two note question
answered by some Jays.

black and white wings flash,
Woodpecker laughs; meanwhile, Cranes
accept offered grain.

between bands of rain,
Ground Doves swirl at sodden seeds,
peek out from long grass.

today, Jay circles,
calling the clouds' thick water;
every ninth wave roars.

Woodpecker answers
Crows' chain of vowels reaching
thick, wet horizon.

six Ducks arc pasture,
too few for formation, fast
against more gray rain.

casting corn circles
results in reciprocal gift;
Blackbird leaves feather.

her speckled chest glows,
she flings herself at Crow yet
Hawk withdraws from kill.

body's betrayal
fast hammer behind sternum;
all is bright, empty.

the hobo Crows know
generous hope; they lurk, wait
for rich offerings.

at the gate, Jay calls,
calls as if hark of return
then more Jays arrive.

they do not migrate
this tribe of Cranes, they homestead;
this is their last stand.

politely they wait
requesting circles of corn;
then, echoing song.

the tree had a stroke,
storm fell nest in withered arm;
Woodpecker calls: grief.

evening in August
last bird Great Snowy Egret
across sky alone.

she is mud-colored,
her mouth yellow; six babies
learn themselves as Ducks.

lone Crow finds millet,
calls tribe long time, long vowels;
horizon: ah-ah.

Crow tribe at horse trough
brother. sister each a turn,
drink; then, all away.

Turkey sisterhood:
noon, little woods in Candler;
too few and distant.

the Cranes come calling;
Crow too calls from power pole:
greeting is distinct.

from hiding, whose voice
this trill as light crests the trees
Blue Bird is it you?

Woodpecker chirrups
throughout the day, a wing flash
maybe at sunset.

sleepless before dawn:
shooting stars, far away Owl
distant but distinct.

midmorning crossing
Payne's Prairie, one bird in flight:
Great Snowy Egret.

aloe vera blooms
four orange pompoms; from each tube
Hummingbird flits, sips.

almost little storm,
pink, peeping Ducks swoop and spook
Ground Doves whir away.

they sing, show themselves:
Buff Hummingbird, Cardinal,
Cranes—"here is my life".

because it's cat month,
afternoon's tight fist of heat
hides even the Crows.

at noon, suddenly,
Tree Swallows, Barn Swallows swarm,
an hour's union.

one lone Pelican
drifts wings where sand meets sea, Gulf,
tide's gentle retreat.

full moon: blue night sweats,
chanting is only frogs, bugs;
then, Owl, before dawn.

songs of the morning:
Pileated Woodpecker,
two Jays back and forth.

with their russet throats
two Swallows knot air until
thunder, mists of rain.

pink blushes gold, gray;
they show themselves by song first,
then wing in high flight.

Crows find corn in rain
unceasing; they shiver plumes,
call family close.

night creeps from tree roots:
with russet chest, banded tail spread,
Hawk glides silently.

breezy afternoon:
prelude to dark season, queue
on fence cow Egrets.

Orion rides slant
horizon, Mar looms compass,
Barred Owl salutes dawn.

noon—mamma Hawk's song:
soprano descending note,
making sure she's heard.

in fading August,
in retreating light, one last
white wings, gray clouds rise.

first hour of light,
later now, yet voices ring:
Crow, Woodpecker, Crane.

Whippoorwill is gone
dark's domain now insects, frogs;
even Owls' call rare.

sun's slant retreats west
ever faithful each other
Cranes visit for corn.

memory's echo:
Pileated Woodpecker;
still one greets morning.

before sun crest trees,
Blue Heron chuckles in flight
away from pink clouds.

one Snowy Egret
alone on the dock, huddles;
tribe of thousands gone.

Cattle Egret jumps,
 then citrus-hued stare, crest up;
a moment, away.

after rain, Cranes come,
despite thunder clouds' slow surf,
trusting corn's gold gift.

Mockingbird returns,
griot of odyssey perched
cypress tree's apex.

September sun's slant:
southerly, buttery, less;
even Hawks hurry.

almost forlorn note
Downy Woodpecker at noon,
hunting vertical.

fingers of arctic,
bright breeze; Black Vulture arcs close
then, tilt of wing, gone.

of morning's voices,
Whistling Ducks' pink peep catches
ever later light.

Tree Swallow poses,
bare branch, lets himself be seen
even preens deep blue.

light crests trees due east;
wing and glint one circle south,
one glimpse: Bald Eagle.

Orion due east:
prodigal, Great Horned Owl's opera
before mist rises.

twilight is long, gray;
Whistling Ducks peep and weave air,
flock of nine, only.

waxing moon rising,
southeast, flock vectors pink clouds
gray to gray oneness.

bright wind smells of ice,
afternoon reddens jasmine,
rowdy Crows parlay.

silences grow long,
voices call briefly to wind,
tribes lost, few remain.

fortnight of lovebugs,
season of cicadas;
midmorning Hawk calls.

full moon equinox:
silver midnight, brief visit,
Owl calls—gratitude.

sunset equinox:
curbside corpse unwanted tree,
rescued; Jay calls yes.

silver sun due east,
retreat to south, yet light calls
Ground Doves, Woodpecker.

Cardinals, a pair,
arc between young live oak trees;
tender peeks, noon mist.

morning rain abates;
Cardinal and grasshopper
curve in unison.

maybe two brothers,
Red-Bellied Woodpeckers, climb;
hunting together.

afternoon after
3am roaring rain storm:
Cardinal's soft voice.

an orange horizon:
air change, woodpeckers—two types—
sound out distinctly.

Inconspicuous,
pale chest against pale clouds,
Red-Tailed Hawk watches.

when shadows walk long,
to return to those waiting:
Horses, Dogs, Cats, Cranes.

indigo goes gray,
Barred Owl sings one silver dirge,
then Rooster's solo.

sun slips sideways south,
shifting shadows, colors: pale,
even Crows distant.

furious, golden,
light crests trees; Blackbird perches,
makes circular song.

Brown-Headed Nuthatch
pauses, gives regard from fence,
flits away to pines.

Lady Cardinal
asks sweetfeed? So sun seeds too,
but Blackbird gives thanks.

morning's golden mist
to listen daily voices
offering their song.

away hundred miles,
over acres of fine grass
two voices: Hawk, Crow.

gold streaks turn silver;
struggling poplar's withered branch
flash of green: Warbler.

pink plumes Muhley grass,
autumn's note, hurricane's tail
seven doves perch wire.

bitter, somber sky
yet Cattle Egrets above
moment's white flower.

Inanna, Momma:
all lonely love your retreat
last Heron even.

later comes the light,
fewer those in tribe of flight:
one Tree Swallow, just.

and each will call out,
as Hawk does, Woodpecker does,
until none are left.

lavender mist slips
late shadows: machines quiet,
so Heron's song heard.

first light before dawn
Pileated Woodpecker
brief soliloquy.

kissing beak to beak,
two Crows aloft power line
in the gray morning.

early evening clouds,
Bluejay, little Woodpecker
fly past in greeting.

this chorus of hope,
from Cardinal, Crane and Crow,
season of mourning.

ripe poke, beauty fruit
excites Grackle's noisy lust;
Warbler bends dark poll.

rain, early twilight,
pairs: Cardinals fly love knots,
Cranes stroll together.

mist lingers 'till noon;
Blackbird sings insistently:
light being, big voice

full moon, October:
tentative, tremolo—Loon
never heard before.

red tail a bright wedge,
Hawk calls out relentlessly
all morning above.

pink east, flare of gold:
Pileated Woodpecker,
Crows robust exchange.

Cooper Hawk seeks thrills:
Surfing air swells in traffic,
low glide, brown gaze calm.

cold creeps metal claws;
darkness grows, brings morning mist;
voice of first light: Crows.

rousted from their roost,
a swirling double helix,
Crows aloft at dawn.

adept sensing air,
Vulture tilts port or starboard,
dark wings extended.

season of shadows,
of Crows, of Vultures, of cold;
gone the sweet voices.

what fortune becomes
Eastern Phoebe sitting silent
all air machine growl.

faithful Cardinals:
gentle, cheerful squeaks; vivid,
flirting; this home yours.

Mother, All Hallow's:
Crows calling sunset sisters,
Doves hunt seeds at dusk.

All Saints: a warm wind;
Hawk calls the morning: Jay—noon;
Crow—the slanting light.

All Souls : rain whispers,
but Crows are bold, one by one,
yelling and staring.

now comes the winter:
no midnight Owls, coyotes howl
for obscures bright stars.

arctic touch at dawn;
corvids: Jays flash blue, argue,
Crows gang chase Vulture.

sun rises south east,
comes wind; lone voice Cardinal,
and Warbler clicks code.

damp morning's voices:
Hawk above swamp, Crows' vowels,
Jay flashes blue, speaks.

visiting Bluebirds,
Phoebe, politely perch wire
moment, then away.

November grinds bones,
has bass vowels; even Blackbird,
even Hawk, harsh words.

more, more empty sky
no wings, no song, just machines
and metallic haze.

still, these small souls pose,
on branch or wire, a moment's
reverence; Phoebe.

almost southernmost
deep gold light, feathers brightest;
light bones aloft yet.

pale, private fog
lone voices, soft echo: Jay,
resilient Crows.

wind promises ice
to Hawk, who replies her note,
as does Blackbird, Crow.

transient Wren waits,
eventually accepts grapes;
gift for gift: her song.

this moment is round;
most faithful the Cardinals,
soft chirp for the now.

Chirp

Note: Some of these have appeared in *Blue Heron Review*, Summer 2014

Poet, Artist and Equestrian, Su Zi is the editor of the Chapbook series *Red Mare*. She lives with her horses in the wilds of Central Florida.

HYSTERICAL BOOKS
TALLAHASSEE, FL 2019

www.ingramcontent.com/pod-product-compliance
Lightning Source LLC
Chambersburg PA
CBHW020702300426
44112CB00007B/479